Martial
History, Forms a
Volume

Kwon Bup

American Power

by
Al Case

AL CASE

Quality Press

Copyright© 2003 Alton H. Case

All rights reserved.

All rights reserved. No part of this book may be reproduced or transmitted in any form or by any means, electronic or mechanical, including photocopying, recording, or by any information storage and retrieval system, without the written permission of the author.

For information regarding this book go to:

MonsterMartialArts.com
or
AlCaseBooks.com

TABLE OF CONTENTS

	introduction	5
1)	Basic One	7
2)	Basic Two	20
3)	intro to Set One	34
4)	Pole Punching	35
5)	Set One	36
6)	Insertion Throws	62
7)	Purpose	65
8)	A Tight Fist is...	68
9)	Mastering Karate	71
10)	History of Kwon Bup	74
11)	Conclusion	77
12)	Introduction to Set Two	78
13)	Set Two	79
14)	Knowing Forms	100
15)	Relax	103
16)	Shock and Lock	106
17)	Depth of Penetration	109
18)	CBMing the Body Part	112
19)	Conclusion	115
20)	Introduction to Kicking Form	116
21)	Kicking Form	117
22)	Stuff About Kicks	146
23)	Energy Patterns	148
24)	How Many Arts?	150
	Conclusion	153

Dedication

The Baron Family

Mike Baron, a true student and a most excellent martial artist, first suggested filming the Monster Martial Arts courses. He set up the studio, worked the camera, and put in some long hours.

But all our work would have failed if his wife, Kay hadn't translated the videos for computer.

If it wasn't for Mike and Kay I wouldn't be in this business today.

Mike is the attacker in the photos of this book, and his son, Tracy, demonstrates the kata and defenses.

Introduction

Kwon Bup is accelerated Karate. It is Karate with a booster attached to it. It makes the body move with precision, and introduces one to classes of techniques which are not made specific in classical karate.

That being said, let me tell you about the Kwon Bup.

In the Kang Duk Won there were seven basic forms, called Kibons. Two of those, Basic One and Basic Two, were of Kwon Bup.

There were also three Sets, but because there were certain redundancies, and because of what I was trying to do at the time (create a Black Belt in one week) I combined two of the Forms.

There was the Kicking Form.

And there was a Stick Set.

Fortunately, I have the original seven sets written down in a notebook, and may, someday, look at documenting those.

But until that day, you have ninety-five per cent of the original in these pages.

There are a few schools teaching Kwon Bup.

I culled the material and taught the original forms to Tom Mann, who lives in Willits, California. He had students, and they have students, and if one lives in Northern California and is curious, they can seek these people out and study. (It is sometimes called Kwan Bup, and this due to an error on my part. I simply spelled it wrong in transmitting it to Tom, at one point, and the error stuck.)

One time I was up at Bob Babich's house, in the Santa Cruz mountains, and I saw a Martial Arts book on his coffee table.

"What's that?" I asked.

"It's a book my instructor gave to me." The title: 'Kwon Bup.'

I glanced through the pages and saw that it had not much to do with the system he was teaching. Also, it was written in Korean.

"What does it say?" I pointed at a page.

Bob shrugged. "I don't know. I don't know the language."

"You don't? But how do you read it?"

He grinned. "I just look at the pictures."

I considered the weighty tome in my hands. "What does Kwon Bup mean?"

"Fist Method."

Hmmm.

"What's the difference between a method and the Way?"

"Is there any difference?" and he shrugged.

Years later, when considering what to name the system I had taken out of the classical Kang Duk Won, I selected Kwon Bup.

Bob passed on a few years ago, and this system is a legacy to the best martial artist I have ever seen. And I have seen many.

I will always remember him, however, not for his skill, but for his politeness. He was the most polite and gentle man I have ever known, and it is this that I wish to emulate.

NOTE: Just to let you know so that you won't become confused, when I first wrote this book I was doing some research into teaching people faster, arranging systems in proper order, and so on. Thus, you will come across sections that seem out of place, but were the sum of my thoughts when I wrote this book.

Also, the photographs were of one my younger students, Tracy Baron, a wonderful martial artist. Unfortunately, his excellent form is distracted by my poor photography.

CHAPTER ONE ~ BASIC ONE

Stand in a Natural Stance.

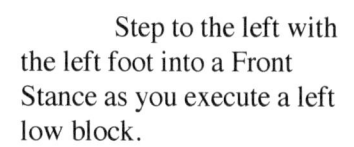

Step to the left with the left foot into a Front Stance as you execute a left low block.

Execute a right reverse punch.

Step forward with the right foot into a Front Stance as you execute a right high block.

Execute a left reverse punch.

Step back with the right foot into an hourglass stance as you protect the face with a left palm block.
Step to the right with the right foot into a front stance as you execute a right low block.

Execute a left reverse punch.

Step forward with the left foot into a front stance as you execute a left high block. Execute a right reverse punch.

Step back with the left foot to a cat stance facing to the front as you execute a right palm block. The left arm prepares to block.

Step forward with the left foot into a front stance as you execute a left low block.

Step forward with the right foot into a front stance as you execute a right punch.

Step forward with the left foot into a front stance as you execute a left punch.

Step forward with the right foot into a front stance as you execute a right punch. KIAI!

Step behind yourself 90 degrees with the left foot as you protect the face with a right palm block.

Step forward with the left foot into a front stance as you execute a left low block.

Execute a right reverse punch.

KWON BUP

Step forward with the right foot into a front stance as you execute a right high block.

Execute a left reverse punch.

Step back with the right foot into an hourglass stance as you protect the face with the left hand.

Step to the right with the right foot into a front stance as you execute a right low block.

Execute a left reverse punch.

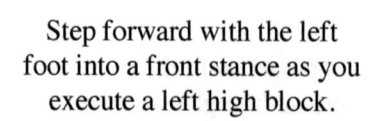

Step forward with the left foot into a front stance as you execute a left high block.

Execute a right reverse punch.

Step back with the right foot into a cat stance as you protect the face with a right palm block.

Step forward with the left foot into a front stance as you execute a left low block.

Step forward with the right foot into a front stance as you execute a punch.

Step forward with the left foot into a front stance as you execute a left punch.

Step forward with the right foot into a front stance as you execute a punch. KIAI!

Step behind yourself with the left foot 90 degrees into a cat stance as you protect your face with a right palm block.

Step to the left with the left foot into a Front Stance as you execute a left low block.

Execute a right reverse punch.

Step forward with the right foot into a Front Stance as you execute a right high block.

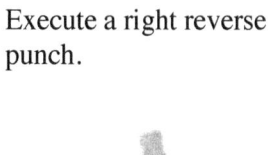

Execute a left reverse punch.

Step back with the right foot into an hourglass stance as you protect the face with a left palm block.

Step to the right with the right foot into a front stance as you execute a right low block.

Execute a left reverse punch.

Step forward with the left foot into a front stance as you execute a left high block.

Execute a right reverse punch. KIAI!

Return with the left foot to the starting position.

CHAPTER TWO ~ BASIC TWO

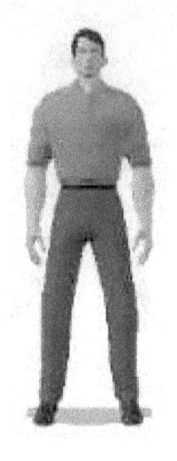

Stand in a Natural Stance.

Step to the left with the left foot into a back stance as you execute a left outward block.

Execute a right reverse punch.

Step forward with the right foot into a back stance as you execute a right inward block.

Execute a left reverse punch.

Step back with the right foot into an hourglass stance as you protect the face with a left palm, and the body with a right dangling forearm block.

Pivot to the right with the right foot into a back stance as you execute a right outward block.

Execute a left reverse punch.

Step forward with the left foot as you execute a left inward block.

Execute a right reverse punch.

Step back with the left foot and face to the front in a cat stance. The right palm protects the face.

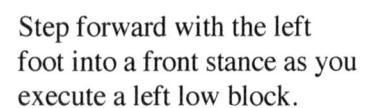

Step forward with the left foot into a front stance as you execute a left low block.

Execute a right reverse punch.

Step forward with the right foot into a front stance as you execute a left reverse punch.

Step forward with the right foot into a front stance as you execute a left reverse punch.

Step forward with the left foot into a front stance as you execute a right reverse punch. KIAI!

Step behind the right foot with the left foot ninety degrees into a cat stance. Execute a right palm block and a left dangling forearm.

Step forward with the left foot into a back stance as you execute a left outward block.

Execute a right reverse punch.

Step forward with the right foot into a back stance as you execute a right inward block.

Execute a left reverse punch.

Step back with the right foot into an hourglass stance. Execute a left palm block and a right dangling forearm block.

Continue turning to the right into a back stance as you execute a right outward block.

Execute a left reverse punch.

Step forward with the left foot into a back stance as you execute a right inward block.

Execute a left reverse punch.

Step to the left with the left foot into a cat stance as you execute a right palm block and a left dangling forearm.

Step forward with the left foot into a front stance as you execute a left low block.

Execute a right reverse punch.

Step forward with the right foot into a front stance as you execute a left reverse punch.

Step forward with the left foot into a front stance as you execute a right reverse punch.

Step forward with the right foot into a front stance as you execute a left reverse punch.

Step behind the right foot with the left foot ninety degrees into a cat stance as you execute a right palm block and a left dangling forearm.

Step to the forward with the left foot into a back stance as you execute a left outward block.

Execute a right reverse punch.

Step forward with the right foot into a back stance as you execute a right inward block.

Execute a left reverse punch.

Step back with the right foot into an hourglass stance as you protect the face with a left palm, and the body with a right dangling forearm block.

Pivot to the right with the right foot into a back stance as you execute a right outward block.

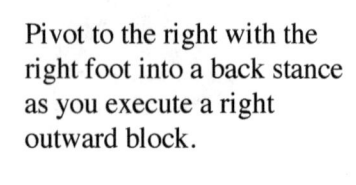

Execute a left reverse punch.

Step forward with the left foot as you execute a left inward block.

Execute a right reverse punch.

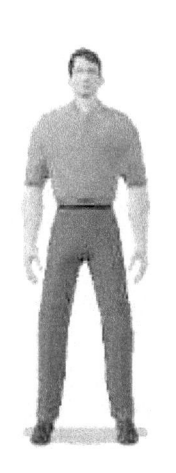

Return with the left foot to the starting position.

CHAPTER THREE ~ INTRODUCTION TO SET ONE

Welcome to the 2nd Black Belt Course.

While other systems have the student learn a couple of Forms, I have you learn an entire system.

I don't want you to just get a little better in one particular line. I want you to get a lot better. And I want you to have some perspective concerning the value of various systems. I also want you to understand that you are not just going for a 2nd Degree Black Belt, you are attempting to Master Karate.

Towards that end I recommend that you take a good, hard look at the Soft side of the Art. Arts such as Tai Chi Chuan, Aikido and Pa Kua Chang, when taught correctly, offer an amazing compliment of knowledge to what you already know.

I also want you to consider teaching. You don't really know something until you get somebody else to learn it.

But most of all I want you to understand one very important item. A Black Belt is an Expert. A Beginning Expert. To properly polish your knowledge and abilities you must understand that you have uncovered only the tip of the ice berg.

A 1st Black Belt is a Beginning Expert, a 2nd Black Belt is an Intermediate Expert, and a 3rd Black Belt is an Advanced Expert.

And an Expert/Expert, a 4th Black Belt, is a Master. So you have a ways to go.

But despair not. In a way, you know how to teach yourself. And with my Expert Instruction you will know what to teach yourself, and you will become a Master in a very short period of time. What took 10 to 12 years in the past can be covered in 1 to 2 years.

Let me offer you one caution, however. Learning, in the Martial Arts, takes on the aspect of inverted geometry.

In the first year of Karate (taught as I have prescribed) the student learns 99% of the Art.

It is easy to think you know it all, at this point. But the truth is that the most important learnings are right ahead. The remaining 1% is what the Art is all about, and that 1% can take 30 years.

The trick is...it's like crawling up the neck of a bottle. The closer you get to the opening the more sky you see. But the more sky you see the tighter the crawl. This is what I mean by inverted geometry. As you progress this will become more and more obvious.

Well, enough yak. Yak belongs in South America, and you belong in this book. So turn the page.

CHAPTER FOUR ~ POLE PUNCHING

The Kwon Bup forms explore certain avenues which you may or may not have touched upon, or at least become aware of. Foremost is the fact of punching from the pole of your leg. This means that the sequence of actions inherent within a punch goes somewhat like this.

1) Weight transfers to one leg, and...

2) Hips turn to line up between the punching arm and the punching leg.

This concept will become more and more obvious as you travel through Kwon Bup.
Enacting this concept purifies the mechanics of the punch, body alignment, grounding the weight, and so forth. Becoming a Black Belt in Outlaw Karate introduced you to CBM. 'Pole Punching' increases Intention, while decreasing effort. Quite simply. when you have mastered Pole Punching the amount of power necessary to an effective punch will be greatly decreased.
Make sure you turn the whole body as you turn the hips from pole to pole.

CHAPTER FIVE ~ SET ONE

Stand naturally, feet just past shoulder width apart, body loose but erect, able to move in any direction at any time, without leaning or otherwise giving hint of direction.

1) Turn the toes slightly in and assume a Sanchin Stance. Prepare the left hand across the body as you execute a right Cross Palm Block.

2) Step to the left with the left foot into a Back Stance (weight right). Simultaneously execute a left Outward Forearm Block.

3) Execute a right Punch as you retract the left arm.

4) Step forward with the left foot into a Front Stance (weight left). Simultaneously execute a left High Block.

5) Execute a right punch as you retract the left arm.

6) Retract the right leg into a Side Cat Stance and prepare to do the sequence to the other side.

7) Step to the right with the right foot into a Back Stance (weight left). Simultaneously execute a right Outward Forearm Block.

8) Execute a left Punch as you retract the right arm.

9) Step forward with the right foot into a Front Stance (weight right). Simultaneously execute a right High Block.

10) Execute a left punch as you retract the right arm.

11) Step to the left with the left leg into a Back Stance (weight right). Execute a left High Knife Block.

12) Execute a right Middle Punch. Execute a pulling motion with the left hand, then curl it into a fist at your side.

13) Execute a left Palm Thrust.

14) Step forward with the right leg into a Back Stance (weight left). Execute a right High Knife Block.

15) Execute a left Middle Punch. Execute a pulling motion with the right hand, then curl it into a fist at your side.

16) Execute a right Palm Thrust.

17) Step forward with the left leg into a Back Stance (weight right). Execute a left High Knife Block.

18) Execute a right Middle Punch. Execute a pulling motion with the left hand, then curl it into a fist at your side.

19) Execute a left Palm Thrust.

20) Step forward with the right leg into a Back Stance (weight left). Execute a right High Knife Block.

21) Execute a left Middle Punch. Execute a pulling motion with the right hand, then curl it into a fist at your side.

22) Execute a right Palm Thrust.

23) Step 90 degrees to the right and turn the body 270 degrees. Prepare the left hand as you execute a right underarm Cross Body Palm Block.

CAMERA ANGLE HAS REVERSED FOR THIS SEQUENCE!

24) Execute a left Double Knifehand Block as you pivot into a Back Stance (weight right).

25) Simultaneously execute a left Palm Down Block and a right horizontal Split Spear- hand. (Split the 3rd and 4th fingers as if spearing two eyes.)

26) Step forward with the left leg into a Front Stance (weight left). Simultaneously execute a right hook as you retract the fist to the hip and a left horizontal Backfist.

27) Retract the left leg into a Sanchin Stance and prepare to do the sequence on the opposite side.

28) Execute a right Double Knifehand Block as you pivot into a Back Stance (weight left).

29) Simultaneously execute a right Palm Down Block and a left horizontal Split Spear-hand. (Split the 3rd and 4th fingers as if spearing two eyes.)

30) Step forward with the right leg into a Front Stance (weight right). Simultaneously execute a left hook as you retract the fist to the hip and a right horizontal Backfist.

31) Step forward and to the left with the left foot into a Back Stance (weight right). Raise the left hand palm out to the side as you execute a right Palm Down Block.

32) Execute a left Inward Middle Block.

33) Execute a right Punch.

34) Step forward right foot into a Back Stance (weight left). Raise the right hand palm out to the side as you execute a left Palm Down Block.

35) Execute a right Inward Middle Block.

36) Execute a right Punch.

37) Step forward with the left foot into a Back Stance (weight right). Raise the left hand palm out to the side as you execute a right Palm Down Block.

38) Execute a left Inward Middle Block.

39) Execute a right Punch.

40) Step forward right foot into a Back Stance (weight left). Raise the right hand palm out to the side as you execute a left Palm Down Block.

41) Execute a right Inward Middle Block.

42) Execute a right Punch.

CAMERA ANGLE IS FROM THE FRONT AGAIN FOR NEXT SEQUENCE.

43) Step 90 degrees to the left with the right foot and turn the body 270 degrees and prepare for the next sequence.

45) Pivot to the left into a Back Stance (weight right) as you execute a left Horizontal Backfist.

46) Step forward with the left leg and start to circle the right hand in front of the face and circle the left hand down past the groin. (46 and 47 are one step)

47) Step into a Horse Stance and finish circling the palms as you execute a left vertical Backfist.

48) Retract the right leg into a Sanchin Stance and prepare to do the sequence on the opposite side.

49) Pivot to the right into a Back Stance (weight left) as you execute a right Horizontal Backfist.

50) Step forward with the right leg and start to circle the left hand in front of the face and circle the right hand down past the groin.

51) Step into a Horse Stance and finish circling the palms as you execute a right vertical Backfist.

52) Retract the right leg to a Natural Stance and end the form.

CHAPTER SIX ~ INSERTION THROWS

An Insertion Throw is that type of throw wherein you insert your structure directly into the weak points of your opponent's structure, thereby causing the collapse of his structure. This is not a throw which utilizes 'Harmony,' although you may find elements of Harmony. This is not a 'Rotary Throw,' though you may find elements of rotation. This is not a throw utilizing Flow. This is a Flow using Force, but when you understand the concept of Insertion you will be surprised at how easily your opponent will fall. Practice aids you in achieving effortlessness.

NOTE: In an Insertion Throw you must project your Intention under the arm, or past the neck, or through the legs, then use the Intention while virtually ignoring the body of your opponent.

FORM APPLICATION #1 OUT-HIGH
(Sorry about the photo.)

The Attacker steps forward with the left leg and punches to the body with the left hand.
The Defender steps back with the left leg into a Back Stance (weight left) and executes a right Outward Block.

The Attacker punches with the right hand to the face. The Defender executes a left High Block.

The Defender shuffles forward, striking the Attacker on the rib cage with his right hand, thus shocking the Attacker (and inserting his Intention under the arm in a straight line forever) so that he can execute an Upper Armlock Insertion.

CHAPTER SEVEN ~ PURPOSE

The purpose of this level is to change you into a machine.

While this sounds a bit ominous, the truth is actually quite enjoyable.

The truth is you learn harmony of a hard sort. You learn to adjust to whatever attack is happening and offer simultaneous blocks and counters.

After this level nothing in the human form of attack will be able to overwhelm you. And the truth is that you will become split second,, State of the Art, polished. Your perceptions will encompass and absorb and whatever Attacks are offered to you will become as commonplace.

So don't dread, go ahead and let the Art become Science.

FORM APPLICATION #2 PULL-HIT

The Attacker steps forward with the right leg and punches to the face with the right hand.

The Defender steps back with the left leg into a Back Stance (weight left) and executes a right High Knife Block.

The Defender grabs the Attacker's wrist and pulls him down with his right hand and punches him in the body with the left h and.

The Defender shuffles forward and executes a hip throw.

CHAPTER EIGHT ~ 'A TIGHT FIST IS...'

I studied with one fellow for seven years, and in that seven years he said maybe a dozen things to me. One of the things he said was 'A tight fist is a heavy fist.' This is true. But what you had to realize is that the secret of making your fist tight is being absolutely loose before and after. Practice being as loose as possible between focus points. Don't make the whole body tight. Tighten only the fist. Let your body become whiplike and explode only the fist in your opponent. This, incidentally, is the secret to creating Internal Power in the Art of Karate. Without this concept of Loose your Karate will never make it to the higher levels. Karate means 'Empty Hands.' Empty Hands are 'Loose Hands.' Do Karate long enough and the Emptiness will spread throughout your whole body. And if your whole body is loose, or empty, and what is empty is light and weightless, then you will understand Karate. Think on this when you make your fist tight.

FORM APPLICATION # 3 KNIFE SPEAR

The Attacker steps forward with the right foot and punches to the body with the right hand.
The Defender steps back with the right leg into a Back Stance and executes a left double Knife Block.

The Attacker punches to the body with the left hand.
The Defender executes a left Palm Down Block and a right Split Spear to the eyes.

Shuffling forward, the Defender hooks the Attacker's left hand with his right hand and places the left hand against the neck (inserting his Intention forever) and executes a Neck Insertion Throw.

CHAPTER NINE ~ MASTERING KARATE

According to the dictionary a Master (noun) is:
1) A man who rules others or has control, authority, or power over something....
2) A person very skilled and able in some work, profession, science, etc.

Also, a Master (verb) is:
1) To become Master of; to conquer; to overpower; to subdue; to bring under control. 2) To rule or govern as Master.
3) To become expert at; as, to master a science.
4) To possess.

So you are striving to do all these things.

FORM APPLICATION #4 PALM DOWN

The Attacker kicks to the groin with the left leg.
The Defender steps back with the right leg into a Back Stance (weight right). Simultaneously he executes a right Palm Down Block.

The Attacker sets the left foot down and punches to the body with the left hand. The Defender executes a left Inward Middle Block.

The Defender grabs the Attacker's left wrist with his right hand and inserts his left arm over the left shoulder of the Attacker and executes a Neck Insertion Takedown.

CHAPTER TEN ~ HISTORY OF KWON BUP

Kwon Bup (Korean) literally translates as 'The Fist Method.' It is the name of the Art you are studying on this level.

Originally it was developed by my Instructor (Bob Babich) and his Black Belts (This was at a school in San Jose called the 'Kang Duk Won.' Kang Duk Won (Korean) literally translates as 'House for Espousing Virtue.')

When it was developed it was merely added on to the Kang Duk Won piecemeal.

Years later, when I began teaching, one of my students (Tom Mann) wanted to teach Karate but, for various reasons, didn't want to teach the entire system of the Kang Duk Won. (NOTE: he had had epiphany and wanted to help people through the martial arts, he had already studied the KDW years before, but had largely forgotten it. I asked him whether he wanted to relearn the Kang Duk Won, or learn the Kwon Bup, which was shorter. He chose Kwon Bup.) At that point I separated the two systems, Kwon Bup and Kang Duk Won, and told him to teach Kwon Bup.

Kwon Bup was a phrase used to describe Martial Arts in Korea some thousands of years in the past. It was also the name of a book given to my Instructor by his instructor (Norman Ra). At one point my Instructor was supposedly 'Outlawed' by the Korean Organizations. At that time he began calling the Kang Duk Won by the name of Kwon Bup. When I culled the Kang Duk Won for the system developed by my Instructor and his students I called the system Kwon Bup.

Over the years, as I studied the progress of my student and his students, I realized the incredible value of Kwon Bup as a unique and separate Art. It was able to stand up quite well on its own two feet. It was, to a greater extend, through this study of Karate systems that I was able to come up with my own brand of Karate, which I call 'Outlaw Karate.'

For reasons which will become apparent as you progress through this course, Kwon Bup becomes an excellent and logical progression of Karate after a student has completed a study of Outlaw Karate. I have boiled the concepts within Kwon Bup from seven forms to three, and certain changes have been made by myself so that the system will progress more smoothly from Outlaw Karate, and so that certain concepts and principles will be more firmly adhered to.

FORM APPLICATION #5 ROLLING BACKFIST

    The Attacker steps forward with the left leg and punches to the body with the left hand.
    The Defender steps back with the left leg into a Back Stance and executes a left Cross Body Palm Block.

    The Defender executes a right horizontal Backfist to the Attacker's face.

The Attacker strikes with his right hand.

The Defender uses a right Rolling Palm to slap the Attacker's hand down and aside.

The Defender grabs the Attacker's right wrist with his left hand and simultaneously sweeps his right arm across the Attacker's neck while sliding into a horse Stance behind the Attacker's left leg.

Stepping forward with the left leg and applying spiral arm motion, will result in an Insertion Throw.

CHAPTER ELEVEN ~ CONCLUSION

I have said there is a difference between learning and knowing. the best way to bridge the difference is to teach. When you are first learning you learn by being the Attacker and by being the Defender. A teacher gets to stand back and control both the Attacker and the Defender. This gives him insights and information far beyond what is available to the student. Besides, this is the first step in learning how to control people (as opposed to destroying), and in learning how to control multiple bodies. Remember, you don't really know something until you get somebody else to know it.

CHAPTER TWELVE ~ INTRODUCTION TO SET TWO

When one CBMs one has become Expert. This means one has entered the Second Level of the Martial Arts. In this system obviously this happens somewhere around the conclusion of the six Forms of Outlaw Karate, at which time one is promoted to First Degree Black Belt.

When one CBMs he becomes aware of the Thoughts behind his Actions.

When one polishes sufficiently one will be able to see the Thoughts behind an opponent's Actions, and has achieved Mastery. This means that one has entered the Third Level of the Martial Arts. In this system this happens somewhere around the conclusion of the Three Forms of Kwon Bup, and the One Form which is the source of True Karate, at which time one is promoted top Fourth Degree Black Belt.

There is more, of course, but this will do for now.

CHAPTER THIRTEEN ~ SET TWO

Ready Position--Stand natural with feet shoulder width apart.

1) Assume Sanchin Stance while looking to the left. Execute a right Cross Palm block under the left arm. Prepare the right arm.

2) Pivot to the left into a Back Stance and execute a left chop.

3) Execute a right Punch under a left Cross Palm Block.

KWON BUP

4) Step forward with the left foot into a Front Stance (weight left) and execute a left Chop.

5) Bring the right foot next to the left in a Sanchin stance and prepare to do sequence on the opposite side.

6) Pivot to the right into a Back Stance and execute a right chop.

7) Execute a left Punch under a right Cross Palm Block.

8) Step forward with the right foot into a Front Stance (weight right) and execute a right Chop.

9) Step to the left with the left foot into a Back Stance. Make a Parry with the right hand and draw it to the side as you circle the left hand up and around to a Low Inward Sweeping Block.

10) Reverse the circle of the left hand to a Cross Palm Block. Simultaneously execute a right Punch under the block.

11) Step forward with the right foot into a Back Stance. Make a Parry with the left hand and draw it to the side as you circle the right hand up and around to a Low Inward Sweeping Block.

12) Reverse the circle of the right hand to a Cross Palm Block. Simultaneously execute a left Punch under the block.

13) Step forward left foot into a Back Stance. Make a Parry with the right hand and draw it to the side as you circle the left hand up and around to a Low Inward Sweeping Block.

14) Reverse the circle of the left hand to a Cross Palm Block. Simultaneously execute a right Punch under the block.

15) Step forward with the right foot into a Back Stance. Make a Parry with the left hand and draw it to the side as you circle the right hand up and around to a Low Inward Sweeping Block.

16) Reverse the circle of the right hand to a Cross Palm Block. Simultaneously execute a left Punch under the block.

17) Step forward with the right foot into a Horse Stance and execute a right Chop.

18) Step 90 degrees to the left with the right foot and turn the body 270 degrees into a Back Stance. Simultaneously execute a right Cross Palm Block and a left Cross Palm block.

CAMERA ANGLE HAS REVERSED HERE!

19) Execute a left Front Heel Kick.

20) Set the left foot down and execute a left Cross Palm Block and a right Punch under the block.

21) Step forward with the left foot and pivot into a horse Stance. simultaneously execute a right High Knife Hand Block and a left Chop.

21) Retract the right foot and turn 180 degrees into a Back Stance. Simultaneously execute a left Cross Palm Block and a right Cross Palm block.

22) Execute a right Front Heel Kick.

23) Set the right foot down and execute a right Cross Palm Block and a left Punch under the block.

24) Step forward with the right foot and pivot into a horse Stance. simultaneously execute a left High Knife Hand Block and a right Chop.

25) Step to the left with the left leg into a Back Stance. Simultaneously execute a right Low Block and a left Inward Middle Block.

26) Step forward with the right leg into a Back Stance. Simultaneously execute a left Low Block and a right Inward Middle Block.

27) Step forward with the left leg into a Back Stance. Simultaneously execute a right Low Block and a left Inward Middle Block.

28) Step forward with the right leg into a Back Stance. Simultaneously execute a left Low Block and a right Inward Middle Block.

29) Shift into a horse Stance and simultaneously execute a left Low Block and a right Inward Middle Block.

30) Pivot into a Front Stance (weight right). Simultaneously retract the left hand to the hip and execute a right Vertical Backfist.

CAMERA ANGLE REVERSE FOR THE NEXT SEQUENCE

31) Step 90 degrees to the left with the right foot into a Sanchin Stance. Simultaneously execute a right Cross Palm Block and prepare the left hand.

32) Pivot to the left into a Back Stance and execute a Single Knife Hand Block.

33) Execute a right Cross Palm Block.

34) Step forward with the left leg into a Horse Stance. Execute a left Punch to the side.

35) Bring the right foot next to the left in a Sanchin Stance and prepare to do the sequence on the opposite side.

36) Pivot to the right into a Back Stance and execute a right Single Knife Hand Block.

37) Execute a left Cross Palm Block.

38) Step forward with the right leg into a Horse Stance. Execute a right Punch to the side.

39) Return to the Natural Stance and end the form.

CHAPTER FOURTEEN ~ KNOWING FORMS

To Learn a Form is to be able to do it.

To know a Form is to be able to use it.

Here are several tricks to help you 'Know' a form.

Do the Form on the opposite side.

Do the form backwards. (Not just reverse sequence, but trace the actual path of the body motions backwards.)

Do the Form while holding weapons.

Do the Form slowly, as if doing Tai Chi.

Do the Form and look for Circle, as if doing Aikido.

And, because the Promised Fight is the bridge between the pure world of Form Theory and the real world of practical application, practice Promised Fights with all these methods.

You see, the trick is in investing your thought into the Form. The Form will only become what you make it. And so will you.

FORM APPLICATION #6 PALM-CHOP

The Attacker steps forward with the left foot and punches to the body with the left hand.

The Defender steps back with the left foot. As he steps he executes a left Underarm Cross Palm Block.

As the Defender sinks his weight into a Back Stance (weight left) he executes a right Chop to the neck.

The Attacker punches to the face with the right hand. The Defender executes a right Cross Palm Block and a left Punch to the body.

The Defender inserts the right arm against the neck and grabs the Attacker's right wrist with his left hand. Using the neck and the arm as levers the Defender steps forward with the left foot and spirals the Attacker to the ground.

CHAPTER FIFTEEN ~ RELAX

The 2nd Level is really all about relaxing. When you can relax in the middle of combat, when the Martial Arts are second nature, you are a Master.

FORM APPLICATION #7 SPLITTING

The Attacker kicks to the groin with his left leg.
The Defender steps back with the left foot into a Back Stance (weight left). Simultaneously he executes a right Low Sweep.

The Attacker sets his left foot forward and punches to the face with his left hand. The Defender executes a right Cross Palm Block and a left Punch.

The Defender places his right arm across the Attacker's neck and slides behind the Attacker in a Horse Stance.

CHAPTER SIXTEEN ~ SHOCK AND LOCK

The following takedown is what I call a Shock and Lock technique. When somebody resists you you have two choices, Force or Flow. If the fellow is too strong, or you have insufficient position, you must flow, that is step around until you have regained superior body position. A study of Pa Kua Chang will enable you to do this.

If you have sufficient body position then you might consider a Shock and Lock. You shock the opponent by striking him so that his attention is no longer on resisting you, but upon the pain in a body part. Then you will find you will be able to perform the Insertion and/or throw.

FORM APPLICATION #8 MID-LOW

The Attacker kicks to the groin with the left leg.

The Defender steps back with the right leg into a Back Stance (weight right). Simultaneously he executes a left Inward Middle Block and a right Low Block.

The Attacker sets his foot forward and punches to the face with his left hand.

The Defender steps forward with the left leg into a Horse Stance. Simultaneously he executers a right High block and a left Hammerfist to the groin.

The Defender inserts his left arm against the Attacker's neck and pushes up on the Attacker's left arm with his right arm.

CHAPTER SEVENTEEN ~ DEPTH OF PENETRATION

When you strike you should either hit flesh, muscle or bone.

Flesh is when you strike your partner in practice and no harm is done.

Muscle is when you strike so that bruises are the result.

Bones is when you purposely break the twigs we call bones.

Depth of penetration depends upon on how deep you can 'feel' with your fist. This is a matter of perception. So let's talk about some real perception and some real penetration. Real penetration deals with finding a particular type of weakness in an opponent. It can also be called how to appear mystical by pounding your opponent into the ground. When you strike you must CBM your strike. As you press your entire weight onto your opponent you will fell his body underhand. Feel his bones wiggle and sway, and search for that part of the body which has the greatest weakness and direct your CBMed weight into that portion of his body.

This could be called 'Unaligning your Opponent's Body Parts,' and usually it is more in line with Tai Chi Chuan teachings, but all Arts usually come to the same end.

FORM APPLICATION #9 DUMPING

The Attacker steps forward with the left leg and punches to the body with the left hand.

The Defender steps back with the left leg into a Back Stance (weight left). Simultaneously he executes a right Single Knife Block.

The Attacker punches to the face with the right hand. The Defender executes a left Cross Palm (guiding) Block.

KWON BUP

The Defender drops into a horse Stance behind the Attacker's legs and lifts the Attacker by the legs.

CHAPTER EIGHTEEN ~ CBM-ING THE BODY PART

CBM-ing the Body Part is when you put the entire weight of the body into a particular body part.

If you are hanging from the edge of a roof you are hanging by your hands, therefore your entire weight rests in your hands.

So why can't you do this with a strike?

FORM APPLICATION #10 BODY SPLITTING

The Attacker steps forward with the left foot and punches to the body with the left hand.

The Defender takes a slight hop to the rear with his left foot and executes a right Stomp to the knee. Simultaneously he hits the elbow with his right hand and the wrist with his left hand, thus break the arm.

The Defender shuffles forward and executes a left Punch to the body while pushing the Attacker's left arm aside.

The Defender ducks his body under the Attacker's left arm and slides into a horse Stance behind the Attacker. (Don't lift your heel to make it work--snug the foot under his stance to make it work).

CHAPTER NINETEEN ~ CONCLUSION

A student once came to a Master and requested a contest. The Master trounced him severely.

The student practiced for two hours a day for two years, then returned to the Master and requested a contest. The Master trounced him worse than before.

The student practiced four hours a day for four years, then returned to the Master and requested a contest. The Master trounced him worse than ever.

"Master!" protested the student. "No matter how many hours a day I practice you just beat me worse and worse.

"You practice hours a day?" replied the Master. "There is no hour when I do not practice."

CHAPTER TWENTY ~ INTRODUCTION TO THE KICKING FORM

Welcome to the 3rd section of the 2nd Black Belt Course.

Your hands should be as strong as your feet. Your feet should be as agile as your hands. You should be able to make the progression from kick to strike to takedown.

But the real question is...how polite are you?

CHAPTER TWENTY-ONE ~ KICKING FORM

Ready Position--Natural Stance.

1) Cross body Palm block with the right hand under the left arm as you move the left foot next to the right in a Cat Stance (weight right).

2) Extend the left leg in a side Thrust to the left. Simultaneously execute a left horizontal palm block.

3) Pivot so that the body is facing to the left and execute a left Front Snap Kick and a left Outward Middle Block.

4) Set the left leg down to the front in a Back Stance (weight right). Simultaneously execute a right Punch.

5) Execute a right Front Snap Kick and a right Cross Body Palm Block.

6) Retract the right leg and reassume the Back Stance (weight right). Simultaneously execute a left Punch.

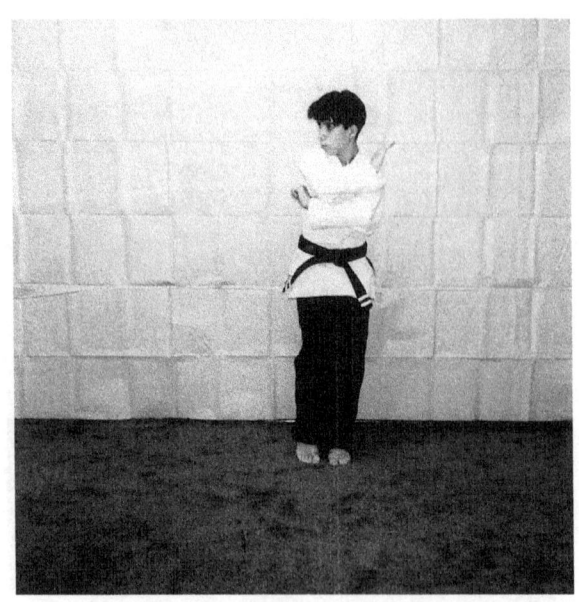

7) Pivot and prepare to do the sequence on the opposite side.

8) Extend the right leg in a side Thrust to the right. Simultaneously execute a right horizontal palm block.

9) Pivot so that the body is facing to the right and execute a right Front Snap Kick and a right Outward Middle Block.

10) Set the right leg down to the front in a Back Stance (weight left). Simultaneously execute a left Punch.

11) Execute a left Front Snap Kick and a left Cross Body Palm Block.

12) Retract the left leg and reassume the Back Stance (weight right). Simultaneously execute a right Punch.

8) Execute a left Side Stomp and a right Cross body Palm Block to the left.

9) Execute a left Wheel Kick and a left Cross body Palm block to the front.

10) Set the left leg forward in a Back Stance (weight right) and execute a right Punch.

11) Execute a right oblique Foot Stomp and a left Cross Body Palm Block to the front.

12) Execute a right Wheel Kick and a right Cross body Palm block to the front.

13) Set the right leg forward in a Back Stance (weight left) and execute a left Punch.

14) Execute a left oblique Foot Stomp and a right Cross Body Palm Block to the front.

15) Execute a left Wheel Kick and a left Cross body Palm block to the front.

16) Set the left leg forward in a Back Stance (weight right) and execute a right Punch.

17) Execute a right oblique Foot Stomp and a left Cross Body Palm Block to the front.

18) Execute a right Wheel Kick and a right Cross body Palm block to the front.

19) Stomp the right foot down in a Front Stance (weight right), replacing the left foot, which moves backwards. Simultaneously execute a right vertical Backfist.

CAMERA REVERSES ANGLE AT THIS POINT

20) Step 90 degrees to the left with the right foot and turn the body 270 degrees into a Cat Stance (Weight right). Simultaneously execute a left Cross Palm Block and prepare the right hand.

21) Execute a left Replacement Side Thrust Kick to the left and a left Horizontal Backfist.

22) Set the left foot forward into a Front Stance (weight left) and execute a left vertical Backfist.

23) Execute a left Replacement Front Snap kick to the front and a left Cross body Palm Block.

24) Left Foot Stomp Replacement and a left Vertical Backfist.

25) Bring the right foot next to the left and prepare to do the sequence on the opposite side.

26) Execute a right Replacement Side Thrust Kick to the right and a right Horizontal Backfist.

27) Set the right foot forward into a Front Stance (weight right) and execute a right vertical Backfist.

28) Execute a right Replacement Front Snap kick to the front and a right Cross body Palm Block.

29) Right Foot Stomp Replacement and a right Vertical Backfist.

30) Execute a left Side Stomp Kick to the left. Simultaneously execute a left horizontal Backfist. (You are now coming back down the center.)

31) Set the left foot down to the front in a Back Stance (weight right). Simultaneously execute a right Punch.

32) Execute a left spear.

33) Execute a right Heel Thrust to the front (sorry, no picture). Simultaneously execute a right horizontal cross palm block. (You are now coming back down the center.)

34) Set the right foot down to the front in a Back Stance (weight left). Simultaneously execute a left Punch.

35) Execute a right spear.

36) Execute a left heel thrust to the front. Simultaneously execute a left cross palm block. (sorry, no picture)

37) Set the left foot down to the front in a Back Stance (weight right). Simultaneously execute a right Punch.

38) Execute a left spear.

39) Execute a right heel thrust to the front. Simultaneously execute a right cross palm block. (Sorry, no picture)

40) Set the right foot down to the front in a Back Stance (weight left). Simultaneously execute a left Punch.

41) Execute a right spear.

CAMERA ANGLE REVERSES

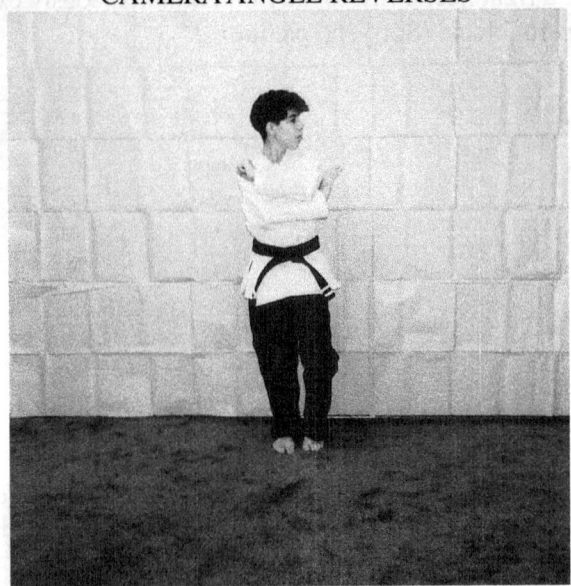

42) Bring the right foot across the body to the left and turn the body 270 degrees into a Cat Stance (weight right). Execute a right underarm Cross Body Palm Block.

43) Execute a left Side Thrust Kick and left Horizontal Backfist.

44) Set the left foot forward in a Front Stance (weight left) and execute a horizontal Backfist.

45) Execute a left Replacement Wheel Kick and a left Cross Body Palm Block.

46) Execute a left Replacement Foot Stomp and a left Horizontal Backfist.

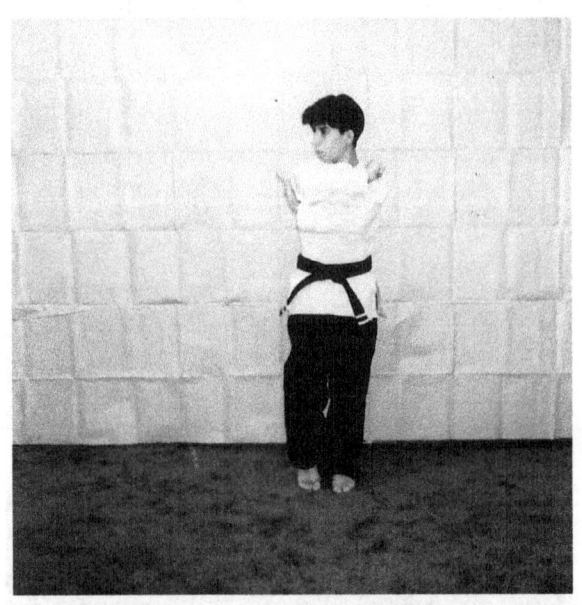

47) Bring the left foot next to the right in a Cat Stance (weight left) and execute a left Cross Palm Block while you prepare the right hand.

48) Execute a right Side Thrust Kick and right Horizontal Backfist.

49) Set the right foot forward in a Front Stance (weight right) and execute a right horizontal Backfist.

50) Execute a right Replacement Wheel Kick and a right Cross Body Palm Block.

51) Execute a right Replacement Foot Stomp and a right Horizontal Backfist.

52) Bring the right foot back and end the form.

CHAPTER TWENTY-TWO ~ STUFF ABOUT KICKS

Techniques gain extra power from sinking downward with the weight. This is why a Replacement Kick is, in addition to being strategically maneuverable, powerful.

And this is why you should bend the support leg upon impact. Not only does it act as a shock absorber, but as a supercharger.

Also, you should use the ball of the foot on the Wheel Kick whenever possible. Aside from being artistically sound, using the ball of the foot provides a more penetrating, smaller surface. It is the difference between using a baseball bat and a hammer.

A high knee increases penetrative power.

When kicking the the Lower Triangle (that triangle utilizing the feet and the One Point as its points must tilt, and the Upper Triangle (above the One Point) must relax.
Body Alignment (and therefore Grounding) must take place from the Grounding Foot to the One Point to the Impact Foot.

Also, you should make a list concerning whether each kick is a vertical kick (for in- stance, the Front Snap Kick) or a horizontal Kick (for instance, the Crescent kick). You should put some thought as to how changing the configuration of the foot necessitates a change in the arc or plane of motion.

Can you CBM your body weight into your foot?

FORM APPLICATION #11 SIDE THRUST

The Attacker steps forward with the right leg and punches to the face with the right hand.

The Defender hops to the left into a Crane Stance while executing a right High Block.

The Defender grabs the attacker's head and pulls it around while kicking to the Attacker's knee with a right Side Thrust kick.

CHAPTER TWENTY-FOUR ~ ENERGY PATTERNS

As you may have realized, Karate is not so much muscles as Energy Patterns.

Muscle wears out. Energy can be created whenever you want it.

The Tan Tien (The One Point) explodes or surges.

The fist, by closing or tightening, creates an explosion within the body of your opponent.

The legs drive connective beams of Energy into the planet, thus creating a Two Pole Energy system.

A block is a ridge of Energy.

And so on.

FORM APPLICATION #12 KICK INSERTION

The Attacker steps forward with the left foot and punches to the face with the left hand.

The Defender executes a left Front Snap Kick and a left Cross Palm Block.

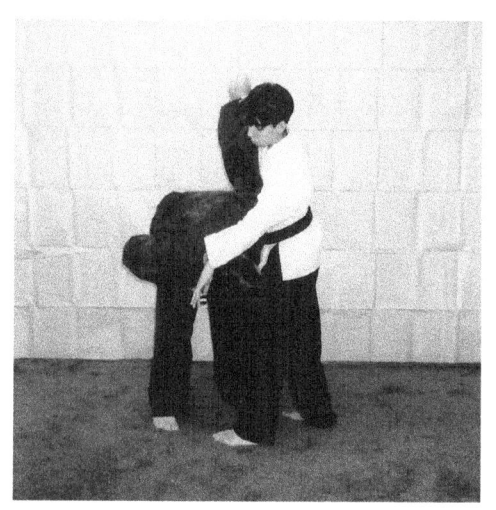

The Defender steps forward, sliding his left hand to the side of the Attacker's neck while grasping the Attacker's wrist with his right hand. Pushing the arm up and around and the neck down the Defender collapses the Attacker.

CHAPTER TWENTY-FIVE ~ HOW MANY ARTS?

How many Arts do you know?

There are those who preach that one only need know one Art, and should spend his life polishing only that one Art.

It is true that virtually all Arts can be extrapolated from one Art, and it is a good idea to have a favorite Art, but the truth of the matter is that you practice your techniques on different people so that you will not be fooled by different body types, and you should practice different Arts for the same reason.

It's a matter of perspective. To fully appreciate the Arts one must look at the movements through a variety of viewpoints. Each Art provides unique viewpoint and dimension to the technique or motion that you are practicing.

So don't stop at one Art.

FORM APPLICATION #13 DOUBLE KICK

The Attacker steps forward with his left leg and punches with the right hand.

The Defender executes a right Cross Palm Block and a left Foot Stomp to the knee. The Attacker punches with the right hand.

The Defender executes a left Cross Palm Block and a left Wheel Kick to the body.

Sliding forward while grasping the Attacker's arm with his right hand, the Defender pulls the Attacker's head back with his left hand.

CONCLUSION

I know I've said this before, but it deserves saying again. In True Karate there is no nationality. In True Karate there is no stylistic difference. And there is no whim or fancy or other interpretation of the Art.

True Karate is based only upon the structures and energies that work.

There can be multitudes of Forms because this is expression, but deviance of a person's individual Form should not occur except in conjunction with the slight deviances of body, and all motions should be structured according to the necessities of analyzing and handling Force and Flow.

If one is willing to understand this, and to let go of the silliness of 'My system is better than yours,' if one is willing to understand principles of physics and mechanics, then one can learn True Karate.

About the Author

Al Case walked into his first martial arts school in 1967. During the Gold Age of Martial Arts he studied such arts as Aikido, Wing Chun, Ton Toi Northern Shaolin, Fut Ga Southern Shaolin, Weapons, Tai Chi Chuan, Pa Kua Chang, and others.

In 1981 he began writing for the martial arts magazines, including Inside Karate, Inside Kung Fu, Black Belt, Masters and Styles, and more.

In 1991 he was asked to write his own column in Inside Karate.

Beginning in 2001 he completed the basic studies of Matrixing, a logic approach to the Martial Arts he had been working on for over 30 years.

2011 he was heavily immersed in creating Neutronics, the science behind the science of Matrixing.

Interested martial artists can avail themselves of his research into Matrixing at MonsterMartialArts.com.

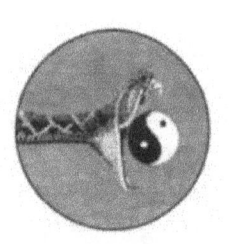

MonsterMartialArts.com

Did you know...

Al Case has written over forty novels?
Go to:

AlCaseBooks.com

Matrixing Kenpo Karate Series!

Matrixing Kenpo Karate
Book One
THE REAL HISTORY
Al Case

Matrixing Kenpo Karate
Book Two
THE SECRET OF FORMS
Al Case

Matrixing Kenpo Karate
Book Three
CREATING A NEW KENPO
Al Case

Pre-Matrixing Series

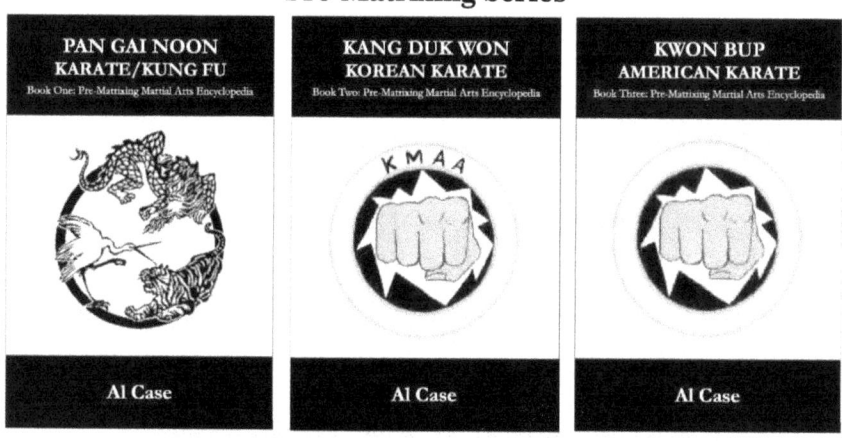

PAN GAI NOON KARATE/KUNG FU
Book One: Pre-Matrixing Martial Arts Encyclopedia
Al Case

KANG DUK WON KOREAN KARATE
Book Two: Pre-Matrixing Martial Arts Encyclopedia
Al Case

KWON BUP AMERICAN KARATE
Book Three: Pre-Matrixing Martial Arts Encyclopedia
Al Case

OUTLAW KARATE BEYOND TRADITIONAL
Book Four: Pre-Matrixing Martial Arts Encyclopedia
Al Case

BUDDHA CRANE KARATE
Book Five: Pre-Matrixing Martial Arts Encyclopedia
Al Case

MARTIAL ARTS BOOKS
On the internet

Advanced Tai Chi Chuan for Real Self Defense!
Black Belt Yoga
Five Martial Arts!
The Last Martial Arts Book (w video links!)
Hidden Techniques of Karate (w video links!)
How to Fix Karate (book one) (w video links!)
How to Fix Karate (book two) (w video links!)
Matrixing Kenpo Karate: Creating a New Kenpo
Matrixing Kenpo Karate: The Real History
Matrixing Kenpo Karate: The Secret of Forms
Neutropia ~ Surrealistic Poetry
The Book of Matrixing
The Book of Neutronics

VIDEO INSTRUCTION
DVDs and downloads at MonsterMartialArts.com

Matrix Karate
Matrix Kung Fu
Matrix Aikido
Master Instructor Course
Shaolin Butterfly
Butterfly Pa Kua Chang
Matrix Tai Chi Chuan
Five Army Tai Chi Chuan
Matrix Tai Chi Chuan
Five Army Tai Chi Chuan
Matrixing Kenjutsu
Blinding Steel (Matrixing Weapons)